You Can't Half Step the 12 Steps

The application of the 12 Steps to every aspect of your life...

Personalize, Memorize, Internalize

To ALL ASPECTS of your life...

Spiritual
Family
Finances
Health
Faith
Substance Abuse (Drug/Alcohol)
Goal Setting

By Linda H. Evans, MA, LLPC

Copyright © 2017 by Linda H. Evans, MA, LLPC

You Can't Half Step the 12 Steps
The application of the 12 Steps to every aspect of your life...
by Linda H. Evans, MA, LLPC

Printed in the United States of America.

ISBN 9781498489188

All rights reserved solely by the author. The author guarantees all contents are original and do not infringe upon the legal rights of any other person or work. No part of this book may be reproduced in any form without the permission of the author. The views expressed in this book are not necessarily those of the publisher.

Scripture quotations taken from the King James Version (KJV) – *public domain*.

www.xulonpress.com

Dedicated to

Mom

I am who I am because of you. Thank you; love you.

Table of Contents

Preface ix

Steps of the Twelve Steps xi

Chapter

1 Personalize, Memorize, Internalize. 13
2 Twelve Steps (Deliverance) 16
3 Spirituality. 24
4 Faith 32
5 Family 39
6 Health 46
7 Finances 53
8 Substances Abuse (Drugs/Alcohol) 59
9 Goal Setting 68

Work Sheets. 80

Preface

This book was not written with the sole purpose of addressing the substance abuse issue or any other addiction you may have. There are thousands of books out there that address those areas specifically. Instead, this book was written as a reminder of who we are as children of God, and the power we have through His Son, Jesus Christ.

Prior to reading this book, I suggest reading Ephesians in your Bible. Reading Ephesians reminds us of what we all possess in Christ. Ephesians reveals the wealth we have in Christ, how we should walk in life, and the warfare we will face. Ephesians is divided into three parts:

1. **Doctrine:** the believers' heavenly calling
2. **Practice:** how the believers should conduct themselves here on earth
3. **Conflict:** the spiritual battle/conflict believers face

Furthermore, it is important to know that the writer of Ephesians, Paul—also known as Saul—was an apostle of Christ Jesus, chosen by the will of God Himself. Paul considered himself to be the worst of the worst, but God still used him. Read Ephesians to understand your position in Jesus Christ and what He can do for you.

Now, on a more personal note, for the past fourteen years I have counseled clients within the criminal justice system. My career started with male juveniles in the early 1990s, and expanded to the adult population, working with both male and females. The adult males and females were inmates, a part of the correctional system. Although my professional career involves working with the criminal population, they all have one thing in common: substance abuse issues. I'm not here to share their stories, but to provide ways to manage life, regardless of what you may be a slave to.

As stated earlier, this is not your typical substance abuse book. You don't have to read to the end to get to the good part. This book will help you apply the twelve principles (twelve steps) to all aspects of your life. Below is a description of my intent for this book.

You Can't Half Step the Twelve Steps; the title speaks for itself. The book is designed to help change the thinking, feelings, beliefs, and behaviors of individuals in order to meet goals in various areas of their lives. The areas I have chosen to focus on are spirituality, family, finances, health, faith, substance abuse, and goal setting. These are my choices, things that are important to me. Once you see how the process works, feel free to apply the principles to any area of your life.

Twelve Steps

One – We admitted that we are powerless over alcohol, and that our lives had become unmanageable.

Two – We came to believe that a Power greater than ourselves could restore us to sanity.

Three – We made a decision to turn our will and our lives over to the care of God as we understood Him.

Four – We made a searching and fearless moral inventory of ourselves.

Five – We admitted to God, to ourselves, and to another human being the exact nature of our wrongdoings.

Six – We were entirely ready to have God remove all these defects of character.

Seven – We humbly asked Him to remove our shortcomings.

Eight – We made a list of all persons we had harmed, and became willing to make amends to them all.

Nine – We made direct amends to such people whenever possible, except when to do so would injure them or others.

Ten – We continued to take a personal inventory, and when we were wrong, we promptly admitted it.

Eleven – We sought, through prayer and meditation, to improve our conscious contact with God as we understood Him, praying only for knowledge of His will for us and the power to carry that out.

Twelve – Having had a spiritual awakening as the result of these steps, we tried to carry this message to alcoholics, and to practice these principles in all our affairs.

The goal of my book is to demonstrate that anyone who makes an honest effort and commit to complete the process of personalizing and memorizing (the internalization of the information takes place on its own) scripture and Twelve Steps associated with your situation, you will improve your life. You can be successful in any area you may struggle with.

Below are examples of various topics you can apply, along with scriptures. There are also simple work sheets to use to get you started. You don't need to have completed or attended an AA/NA program to be a success. All I suggest is applying these simple tools.

Topic Index/Suggested Scriptures

Anxiety	Philippians 4:6-7
Anger	Ephesians 4:32
Family	Acts 16:31
Fear	Hebrew 13:6
Faith	Hebrew 11:1
Divorce	Romans 7:2-3
Weight Control	Proverb 18:20

1

Personalize, Memorize, Internalize

The process to making things happen or changing things in your life starts with personalizing, memorizing, and internalizing. Before going any further, you need to understand each of these key words. Knowing the definitions and how they relate to each other, makes the process possible.

Personalize: Belonging to the individual; to apply to you.

Memorize: To learn something so as to know it from memory.

Internalize: To learn; to absorb into the mind. To make statements or thoughts a part of your thinking.

Personalize: what exactly does this mean? How do you *personalize* the twelve steps to your life? How do you personalize Scripture to your life? First, let's take a look at what *personalizing* is. Personalizing is to make something personal for yourself, to make it yours. When you make something personal, having it belong to you, you use "I," "my," and "me" statements. For example, if you were working on memorizing the first step of the twelve steps, your statement would look something like this:

> **I** have admitted that **I** am powerless over (insert your issue), and my life has become unmanageable.

Using "**I**" statements makes it yours.

Memorize: what exactly does this mean? How do I commit information to my memory? How is committing this information going to help me in my recovery and the other aspects of my life? Let me start off by saying that your mind is the most powerful tool there is. What you put in it will make you stronger. Remember the old saying, "Knowledge is power"? This is so true. Without memory, our knowledge base is limited. You must have the knowledge available for implementation. We will come back to implementation later.

To memorize, as stated above, is to commit to memory; the power or act of remembering something; storing information in the mind. Memorizing information can cause a total transformation for an individual. We have our natural memory, which is just that: natural. We naturally remember certain things throughout our lives, and thus they become a part of us. We operate or make decisions based on things we know or remember. When you commit something to your memory, it is filed away for later use. You will be able to recall or retrieve it at a later time.

There are several different techniques that can be used to effectively enhance our natural ability to memorize. While this book is not written to teach memorization techniques, understand that through memorizing, you *internalize* information. This brings me to the next point.

When you *internalize,* as stated above, you absorb an idea, opinion, or belief, and make it a part of how you think and feel; you make it a part of your knowledge base. Internalizing information can change your attitude and the way you think. This is also referred to as cognitive behavioral therapy. Internalized information becomes a part of your belief system and thinking patterns. You are absorbing new information into your mind, thus *renewing* your mind. The information is being absorbed into the mind and heart.

I mentioned **implementation** earlier, and I want to briefly discuss what it means. Implementation means to carry into effect, to put into action, or to accomplish. This is where most fall short in achieving their goals. Most fail to implement the action steps needed to achieve their goals. But all is not lost. If you follow the process of personalizing and memorizing, internalizing is automatic. You will activate the power you have within. In Ephesians 3:16, Paul states, "that He would grant you, according to the riches of His glory, to be strengthened with might through His Spirit in the inner man" (NKJV). You have been made strong with His power. You can do this!

2

Twelve Steps (Deliverance)

When it comes to the Twelve Steps, think back to the title of the book: *You Can't Half Step the Twelve Steps*. The Twelve Steps are a critical part of your recovery, and you must commit to being disciplined in working on them continuously. My clients often make statements that AA or NA does not work for them, such as, "I can't stand listening to the war stories," or "I am not getting anything from the meetings." They feel forced to attend by their parole or probation agent, which they feel is unfair. Such statements are excuses. Responses such as these often tell me that the individual may not be ready, and it is vital to be ready before beginning the process. I also believe that they are not separating the principles (Twelve Steps) from the meetings themselves, nor practicing the steps in their entirety. You cannot be lukewarm (half stepping) about your recovery. Once an individual has run out of excuses, hit rock bottom, or become just plain tired of the lifestyle, then and only then are they ready for change. The principles of AA or NA will now work.

Twelve Steps (Deliverance)
Scriptures

Psalm 46:1 (NKJV)

"God is our refuge and strength, a very present help in trouble."

Psalm 55:16 (NKJV)

"As for me, I will call upon God, and the Lord shall save me."

Psalm 55:18 (NKJV)

"He has redeemed my soul in peace from the battle that was against me."

Psalm 107:6 (NKJV)

"Then they cried out to the Lord in their trouble, and He delivered them out of their distresses."

Psalm 107:20 (NKJV)

"He sent His word and healed them, and delivered them from their destructions."

Isaiah 41:13 (NKJV)

"For I, the Lord your God, will hold your right hand, saying to you, 'Fear not I, will help you."

Joel 2:32 (NKJV)

"And it shall come to pass that whoever calls on the name of the Lord shall be saved."

Steps of the Twelve Steps

Here is how it works:

One – We admitted that we are powerless over alcohol, and that our lives had become unmanageable.

Two – We came to believe that a Power greater than ourselves could restore us to sanity.

Three – We made a decision to turn our will and our lives over to the care of God as we understood Him.

Four – We made a searching and fearless moral inventory of ourselves.

Five – We admitted to God, to ourselves, and to another human being the exact nature of our wrongdoings.

Six – We were entirely ready to have God remove all these defects of character.

Seven – We humbly asked Him to remove our shortcomings.

Eight – We made a list of all persons we had harmed, and became willing to make amends to them all.

Nine – We made direct amends to such people whenever possible, except when to do so would injury them or others.

Ten – We continued to take a personal inventory, and when we were wrong, we promptly admitted it.

Eleven – We sought, through prayer and meditation, to improve our conscious contact with God as we understood

Him, praying only for knowledge of His will for us and the power to carry that out.

Twelve – Having had a spiritual awakening as the result of these steps, we tried to carry this message to alcoholics, and to practice these principles in all our affairs.

Personalized

To start you off, I will be using myself as an example to demonstrate the use and implementation of Scripture and the Twelve Steps to all areas in my life. Use whatever will work for you; search the Scriptures and use whatever applies in your given situation. Allow the Holy Spirit to guide you and work through you.

As stated above, personalizing is a process by which you make something personal for yourself. You use "I," "my," and "me" statements.

Scriptures (Personalized)

Psalm 46:1 (NKJV)

"God is our refuge and strength, a very present help in trouble."

PERSONALIZED: God is my refuge and strength, a very present in trouble.

Psalm 55:16 (NKJV)

"As for me, I will call upon God, and the Lord shall save me."

PERSONALIZED: As for me, I will call upon God, and the Lord shall save me.

Psalm 55:18 (NKJV)

"He has redeemed my soul in peace from the battle that was against me."

PERSONALIZED: God has redeemed my soul in peace from the battle that was against me.

Psalm 107:6 (NKJV)

"Then they cried out to the Lord in their trouble, and He delivered them out of their distresses."

PERSONALIZED: I called out to the Lord in my trouble, and He delivered me out of my distresses.

Psalm 107:20 (NKJV)

"He sent His word and healed them, and delivered them from their destruction."

PERSONALIZED: He sent His word and healed me, and delivered me from my destruction.

Isaiah 41:13 (NKJV)

"For I, the Lord your God, will hold your right hand, saying to you, 'Fear not, I will help you.'"

PERSONALIZED: The Lord my God will hold my right hand, saying to me, "Fear not, I will help you."

Joel 2:32 (NKJV)

"And it shall come to pass that whoever calls on the name of the Lord shall be saved."

Personalized: And it shall come to pass that when I call on the name of the Lord, I shall be saved.

Steps of the Twelve Steps (Personalized)

One – We admitted that we are powerless over our addiction, and that our lives had become unmanageable.

PERSONALIZED: I admit that I am powerless over the learning of the **Twelve Steps**, and that my life has become unmanageable.

Two – We came to believe that a Power greater than ourselves could restore us to sanity.

PERSONALIZED: I have come to believe that only a Power that is greater than me can empower me to complete the twelve steps.

Three – We made a decision to turn our will and our lives over to the care of God as we understand Him.

PERSONALIZED: I have made a decision to turn my will and my life over to the care of God as I understand Him to be.

Four – We made a searching and fearless moral inventory of ourselves."

PERSONALIZED: I have made a searching and fearless moral inventory of myself.

Five – We admitted to God, to ourselves, and to another human being the exact nature of our wrongdoings.

PERSONALIZED: I have admitted to God, myself, and another human being the exact nature of my wrongdoings.

Six – We were entirely ready to have God remove all these defects of character.

PERSONALIZED: I am ready to have God remove all defects of my character.

Seven – We humbly asked Him to remove our shortcomings.

PERSONALIZED: I have humbly asked Him to remove my shortcomings.

Eight – We made a list of all persons we had harmed, and became willing to make amends to them all.

PERSONALIZED: I have made a list of all persons who I have harmed, and am willing to make amends to all.

Nine – We made direct amends to such people whenever possible, except when to do so would injure them or others.

PERSONALIZED: I will make amends to each person whenever it is possible, except in cases where to do so would cause more injury to the person in question or other people.

Ten – We continued to take a personal inventory, and when we were wrong, we promptly admitted it.

PERSONALIZED: I will continue to take a personal inventory, and when I am wrong, I will promptly admit it.

Eleven – We sought, through prayer and meditation, to improve our conscious contact with God as we understood Him, praying only for knowledge of His will for us and the power to carry that out.

PERSONALIZED: I will seek prayer and meditation in order to improve my relationship with God as I understand Him, praying for knowledge of His will for me and the power to carry it out.

Twelve – Having had a spiritual awakening as the result of these steps, we tried to carry this message to alcoholics, and to practice these principles in all our affairs.

PERSONALIZED: All eleven steps have provided a spiritual awakening, and as a result, I have made it my mission to bring the message of recovery to others and to practice these principles in everything I do.

Memorize

Memorizing is a process that takes practice. Don't give up.

Internalizing is happening

Motivational Thought

We as humans are literally what we think. Our character is a complete sum of our thoughts. What we think is what is in our hearts.

3

Spirituality

This section of my book is the most important. Without Christ Jesus, my Lord and Savior, none of this would be possible. As you seek healing, you cannot ignore your spiritual growth. All of the hundreds of addicts who I have worked with seem to agree that change is possible, but that it requires at least two things. First, you have to want to change, and secondly, that change is internal. So regardless of what your higher power is, your recovery starts from the inside. Our spiritual growth or journey is a process that happens throughout our lives. As we nurture and cultivate the relationship, change happens.

Now, recovery does not happen in a day or overnight, it is an on going process, just as our relationship with God or whoever your higher power may be. Once you have surrendered your life to Him, you will come to realize that you need to seek Him in everything you do.

Think a moment about your earthly relationships and what you do to strengthen them. Our relationship with Him is no different. Talk to the Lord throughout your day in all tasks you do. Speak to Him, and let Him know how things are going. Matthew 6:33 states, "But seek first the kingdom of God and His righteousness, and all these things will be added to you" (NKJV). This must be a priority in your life; without it, you may never know what you can accomplish.

Spirituality

Scriptures

Jeremiah 29:13 (NKJV)

"And you will seek Me and find Me, when you search for Me with all your heart."

Matthew 21:22 (NKJV)

"And whatever things you ask in prayer, believing, you will receive."

Mark 11:24 (NKJV)

"Therefore I say to you, whatever things you ask when you pray, believe that you receive them, and you will receive them."

John 14:13 (NKJV)

"And whatever you ask in My name, that I will do, that the Father may be glorified in the Son."

John 16:24 (NKJV)

"Until now you have asked nothing in My name. Ask, and you will receive, that your joy may be full."

Romans 8:11 (NKJV)

"But if the Spirit of Him who raised Jesus from the dead dwells in you, He who raised Christ from the dead will also give life to your mortal bodies through His Spirit who dwells in you."

Philippians 4:6 (NKJV)

"Be anxious for nothing, but in everything by prayer and supplication, with thanksgiving, let your requests be made known to God."

Steps of the Twelve Steps

One – We admitted that we were powerless over alcohol, and that our lives had become unmanageable.

Two – We came to believe that a Power greater than ourselves could restore us to sanity.

Three – We made a decision to turn our will and our lives over to the care of God as we understood Him.

Four – We made a searching and fearless moral inventory of ourselves.

Five – We admitted to God, to ourselves, and to another human being the exact nature of our wrongs.

Six – We were entirely ready to have God remove all the defects of our character.

Seven – We humbly asked Him to remove our shortcomings.

Ten – We continued to take a personal inventory, and when we were wrong, we promptly admitted it.

Eleven – We sought, through prayer and meditation, to improve our conscious contact with God as we understood Him, praying only for knowledge of His will for us and the power to carry that out.

Personalize

As stated above, personalizing is a process by which you make something personal for yourself. When you make it personal, having it belong to you, you use "I," "my," and "me" statements. For example, if you were working on personalizing scriptures associated with spirituality, it could look something like this:

Scriptures (Personalized)

Jeremiah 29:13 (NKJV)

"And you will seek me and find me, when you search for Me with all your heart."

PERSONALIZED: I will seek Him and find Him, when I search for Him with all my heart.

Matthew 21:22 (NKJV)

"And whatever things you ask in prayer, believing, you will receive."

PERSONALIZED: Whatever I ask for in prayer, I believe I will receive.

Mark 11:24 (NKJV)

"Therefore I say to you, whatever things you ask when you pray, believe that you will receive them and you will have them."

PERSONALIZED: Whatever I ask for in prayer, I believe that I have received it, and it is mine.

John 14:13 (NKJV)

"And whatever you ask in My name, that I will do, that the Father may be glorified in the Son."

PERSONALIZED: Whatever I ask in the name of Jesus, this He will do, that the Father may be glorified in the Son.

John 16:24 (NKJV)

"Until now you have asked nothing in My name. Ask, and you will receive, that your joy may be full."

PERSONALIZED: Until now I have asked nothing in the name of Jesus. If I ask, I will receive, that my joy may be full.

Romans 8:11 (NKJV)

"But if the Spirit of Him who raised Jesus from the dead dwells in you, He who raised Christ from the dead will also give life to your mortal bodies through His Spirit who dwells in you."

PERSONALIZED: If the Spirit of Him who raised Jesus from the dead dwells in me, He who raised Christ from the dead will also give life to my mortal body through His Spirit who dwells in me.

Philippians 4:6 (NKJV)

"Be anxious for nothing, but in everything by prayer and supplication, with thanksgiving let your requests be made known to God."

PERSONALIZED: I should not be anxious about anything, but about everything by prayer and supplication, with thanksgiving let my request be made known to God.

Steps of the Twelve Steps (Personalized)

One – We admitted that we were powerless over alcohol, and that our lives had become unmanageable.

PERSONALIZED: I admit that I am powerless over my **spiritual growth**, and that my life has become unmanageable.

Two – We came to believe that a Power greater than ourselves could restore us to sanity.

PERSONALIZED: I have come to believe that only a Power that is greater than myself can restore me to sanity.

Three – We made a conscious decision to turn our will and our lives over to the care of God as we understood Him.

PERSONALIZED: I have made a conscious decision to turn both my will and my life over to God in my understanding of who God is.

Four – We made a searching and fearless moral inventory of ourselves.

PERSONALIZED: I have made a searching and fearless moral inventory of myself.

Five – We admitted to God, to ourselves, and to another human being the exact nature of our wrongs.

PERSONALIZED: I have admitted to God, myself, and to another person the exact nature of my wrongs.

Six – We were entirely ready to have God remove all of these defects of character.

PERSONALIZED: I am ready to have God remove all defects of my character.

Seven – We humbly asked Him to remove our shortcomings.

PERSONALIZED: I humbly ask God to remove my shortcomings.

Ten – We continued to take personal inventory, and when we were wrong, we promptly admitted it.

PERSONALIZED: I continue to take a personal inventory of myself, and when I am wrong, I promptly admit it.

Eleven – We sought, through prayer and meditation, to improve our relationship with God in order for **His will** to be more effectively carried out in our lives.

PERSONALIZED: I have sought, through prayer and meditation, to improve my relationship with God in order for **His will** to be more effectively carried out in my life.

Memorize

Using your own chosen method of memorization, go ahead and start the process. When I use the method of writing, I write the entire statement or phrase on Post-its or index cards, and write them over and over again, reciting them out loud. Again, do what you feel will work best for you to commit the information to your long-term memory. Once you have done this, you will be able to recall it, with the help of the Holy Spirit.

Internalize

Internalizing is a process of learning. To learn is to absorb internalized statements into the mind, through the process of personalizing and memorizing. The way that you think is ultimately changed as well; this, of course, will also change the way you behave.

Remembering and understanding is a process, and it will take commitment and time. You will only get out of the process what you put into it. When you personalize and memorize the information, it becomes a part of you.

Motivational Thought

Life is a journey, despite the mistakes we have made; today is a new day with a new start.

4

Faith

Faith is defined as having a strong belief in God or in the doctrines of a religion, based on spiritual belief. Some people trust in God, while others trust in money, friends, themselves, political leaders, astrology, fortune tellers, etc. When I struggle in this area, I stay in prayer. We know that according to Hebrews 11:1, "faith is the substance of things hoped for, the evidence of things not [yet] seen" (NKJV). Romans 10:17, states, "So then faith comes by hearing, and hearing by the word of God" (NKJV). When you want your faith to grow, read His Word, and look back on situations that He has seen you through. We, as His children, are to trust and obey. It is in the truth of His Word that the Holy Spirit builds our faith. The Word and the Spirit work together.

Faith

Scriptures

Hebrews 11:1 (NKJV)

"Now faith is the substance of things hoped for, the evidence of things not seen."

Matthew 9:29 (NKJV)

"Then He touched their eyes, saying, 'According to your faith let it be to you.'"

Matthew 9:22 (NKJV)

"But Jesus turned around, and when He saw her He said, 'Be of good cheer, daughter; your faith has made you well.' And the woman was made well from that hour."

Matthew 21:21 (NKJV)

"So Jesus answered and said to them, 'Assuredly, I say to you, if you have faith and do not doubt, you will not only do what was done to the fig tree, but also if you say to this mountain, 'Be removed and cast into the sea,' it will be done."

Mark 11:22 (NKJV)

"So Jesus answered and said to them, 'Have faith in God.'"

Galatians 2:20 (NKJV)

"I have been crucified with Christ; it is no longer I who live, but Christ lives in me; and the life which I now live in the flesh I live by faith in the Son of God, who loved me and gave Himself for me."

Galatians 5:22 (NKJV)

"But the fruit Spirit is love, joy, peace, longsuffering, kindness, goodness, faithfulness."

Steps of the Twelve Steps

One – We admitted that we were powerless over alcohol, and that our lives had become unmanageable.

Two – We came to believe that a Power greater than ourselves could restore us to sanity.

Three – We made a decision to turn our will and our lives over to the care of God as we understood Him.

Four – We made a searching and fearless moral inventory of ourselves.

Five – We admitted to God, to ourselves, and to another human being the exact nature of our wrongs.

Six – We were entirely ready to have God remove all these defects of character.

Seven – We humbly ask God to remove our shortcomings.

Ten – We continued to take a personal inventory, and when were wrong, we promptly admitted it.

Eleven – We sought, through prayer and meditation, to improve our conscious contact with God as we understand Him, praying only for knowledge of His will for us and the power to carry it out.

Personalize

Scriptures (Personalized)

Hebrews 11:1 (NKJV)

"Now faith is the substance of things hoped for, the evidence of things not seen."

PERSONALIZED: What is faith? It is the confident assurance that what I hope for is going to happen. It is the evidence of things I cannot yet see.

Matthew 9:29 (NKJV)

"Then he touched their eyes, saying, "According to your faith let it be to ."

PERSONALIZED: Then He touched my eyes and said, "Because of your faith, it will happen."

Matthew 9:22 (NKJV)

"But Jesus turned around, and when He saw her He said, 'Be of good cheer, daughter; your faith has made you well.' And the woman was made well from that hour."

PERSONALIZED: Jesus turned around and said to me, "Be of good cheer, daughter; your faith has made you well." And I was healed at that hour.

Matthew 21:21 (NKJV)

"So Jesus answered and said to them, 'Assuredly, I say to you, if you have faith and do not doubt, you will not only do what

was done to the fig tree, but also if you say to this mountain, 'Be removed and cast into the sea,' it will be done."

PERSONALIZED: Then Jesus told me, "I assure you, if you have faith and don't doubt, you can do things like this and much more. You can even say to this mountain, 'Be removed and cast into the sea,' and it will be done."

Mark 11:22 (NKJV)

"So Jesus answered and said to them, 'Have faith in God.'"

PERSONALIZED: Then Jesus said to me, "Have faith in God."

Galatians 2:20 (NKJV)

"I have been crucified with Christ; it is no longer I who live, but Christ lives in me; and the life which I now live in the flesh I live by faith in the Son of God, who loved me and gave Himself for me."

PERSONALIZED: I have been crucified with Christ; it is no longer I who live, but Christ lives in me, and the life which I now live in the flesh I live by faith in the Son of God, who loved me and gave Himself for me.

Galatians 5:22 (NKJV)

"But the fruit of the Spirit is love, joy, peace, longsuffering, kindness, goodness, faithfulness."

PERSONALIZED: The fruit of the Holy Spirit is love, joy, peace, longsuffering, kindness, goodness, and faithfulness.

Steps of the Twelve Steps (Personalized)

One – We admitted that we were powerless over alcohol, and that our lives had become unmanageable.

PERSONALIZED: I admit that I am powerless over my **faith** growth, and that my life has become unmanageable.

Two – We came to believe that a Power greater than ourselves could restore us to sanity.

PERSONALIZED: I have come to believe that only a Power that is greater than me can restore me to sanity.

Three – We made a decision to turn both our will and our lives over to the care of God as we understood Him.

PERSONALIZED: I have made a conscious decision to turn both my will and my life over to God as I understand who God is.

Four – We made a searching and fearless moral inventory of ourselves.

PERSONALIZED: I have made a very thorough and fearless moral inventory of who I am.

Five – We admitted to God, to ourselves, and to another human being the exact nature of our wrongs.

PERSONALIZED: I have admitted to God, myself, and to another person the wrongs of my situation.

Six – We were entirely ready to have God remove all these defects of character.

PERSONALIZED: I am ready for God to rid me of all my character defects.

Seven – We humbly ask God to remove our shortcomings.

PERSONALIZED: I humbly ask God to remove my shortcomings.

Ten – We continued to take personal inventory, and when we were wrong, we promptly admitted it.

PERSONALIZED: I continue to take a personal inventory of myself, and when I am at fault, I am willing to admit it.

Eleven – We sought, through prayer and meditation, to improve our conscious contact with God as we understood Him, praying only for knowledge of His will for us and the power to carry that out.

PERSONALIZED: I have sought, through prayer and meditation, to improve my relationship with God in order for **His will** to be more effectively carried out in my life.

Memorize

Keep the process simple: Keep It Simple Stupid (KISS).

Internalizing is happening

Motivational Thought

Internalize the fact that you need to use God's Word to fight against condemning feelings or doubts whenever they occur.

5

Family

Today, the word *family* is defined in many ways. But family is not really defined by what society says it should be. Family is not defined by the cultural norms of the 50s or 60s. We live in an age when many families are headed by single parents (often women), persons of the same gender, and extended persons of the family (neighbors, friends, and other family members).

Regardless of what makes up a family, families are still broken. Two of the main contributors to broken families are death and divorce. Usually when situations change the dynamics of a family, persons within the community will step in to offer the emotional, maturing, and stabilizing influence that the family may need. Regardless of the dynamics, we are to honor our father and mother. According to Exodus 20:12 "Honor your father and your mother, that your days may be long upon the land which the Lord your God is giving you."(NKJV). We honor our parents because we understand that we did not come forth into this world from nothing. We come to understand that our lives have been shaped by those who have raised us. Some of us were raised in fairly stable environments, and others have not. Despite the circumstances, unless we honor the influence of what they have brought to our lives, it will be difficult to move into the future and create the lives we desire.

Now, I too have had family issues to deal with. Coming from seven children in one household, one can only imagine the issues that arose for us. We dealt with everything from sibling rivalry to drugs and incarceration. All of my siblings have had their own issues to deal with. Our family may appear to be dysfunctional, but we all have kept the scriptures listed below in the forefront and have always treated each other with care and concern. The application of these scriptures to my own life has allowed me to make my life what I desired it to be.

Family

Scriptures

Exodus 20:12 (NKJV)

"Honor your father and your mother, so that you may live long in the land the Lord your God is giving you."

Psalm 127:3 (NKJV)

"Behold children are a heritage from the Lord, the fruit of the womb is a reward."

Proverbs 1:8 (NKJV)

"My son, hear the instruction of your father, And do not forsake the law of your mother;"

Ephesians 6:1–2 (NKJV)

"Children, obey your parents in the Lord, for this is right. 'Honor your father and mother'—which is the first commandment with a promise."

Colossians 3:20 (NKJV)

"Children, obey your parents in all things, for this is well pleasing to the Lord."

1 Timothy 3:4 (NKJV)

"one who rules his own house well, having his children in submission with all reverence."

1 Timothy 3:5 (NKJV)

"For if a man does not know how to rule his own house, how will he take care of the church of God?"

Steps of the Twelve Steps

One – We admitted that we were powerless over alcohol, and that our lives had become unmanageable.

Two – We came to believe that a Power greater than ourselves could restore us to sanity.

Three – We made a decision to turn our will and our lives over to the care of God as we understood Him.

Five – We admitted to God, to ourselves, and to another human being the exact nature of our wrongs.

Six – We were entirely ready to have God remove all these defects of our character.

Seven – We humbly ask Him to remove our shortcomings.

Personalize

Scriptures (Personalized)

Exodus 20:12 (NKJV)

"Honor your father and your mother, so that you may live long in the land the Lord your God is giving you."

PERSONALIZED: I will honor my father and mother, so that I may live long in the land the Lord my God is giving me.

Psalms 127:3 (NKJV)

"Behold children are a heritage from the Lord, The fruit of the womb is a reward."

PERSONALIZED: My child is a gift from the Lord; he is a reward from Him.

Proverbs 1:8 (NKJV)

"My son, hear the instruction of your father, And do not forsake the law of your mother."

PERSONALIZED: I will listen to my father's instruction and will not forsake my mother's teaching.

Ephesians 6:1–2 (NKJV)

"Children, obey your parents in the Lord, for this is right. 'Honor your father and mother'—which is the first commandment with a promise."

PERSONALIZED: I will obey my parents in the Lord, for this is right. "I will honor my father and mother"—which is the first commandment with a promise.

Colossians 3:20 (NKJV)

"Children, obey your parents in all things, for this is well pleasing to the Lord."

PERSONALIZED: I will obey my parents in everything, for this pleases the Lord.

1 Timothy 3:4 (NKJV)

"one who rules his own house well, having his children in submission with all reverence."

PERSONALIZED: I must manage my own family well, with children who respect and obey me.

1 Timothy 3:5 (NKJV)

"For if a man does not know how to rule his own house hold, how can he take care of the church of God."

PERSONALIZED: If I cannot manage my own household, how can I take care of God's church?

Steps of the Twelve Steps (Personalized)

One – We admitted we were powerless over alcohol, and that our lives have become unmanageable.

PERSONALIZED: I admit that I am powerless over my **family relationships**, and that they have become unmanageable.

Two – We came to believe that a Power greater than ourselves could restore us to sanity.

PERSONALIZED: I have come to believe that only a Power that is greater than me can restore my **relationships**.

Three – We made a decision to turn our will and our lives over to the care of God as we understood Him.

PERSONALIZED: I have made a decision to turn both my will and my life over to God as I understand Him to manage my **family relationships**.

Five – We admitted to God, to ourselves, and to another human being the exact nature of our wrongs.

PERSONALIZED: I have admitted the reality of the situation to God, myself, and another person.

Six – We were entirely ready to have God remove all these defects of character.

PERSONALIZED: I am ready to have God remove all my defects of character.

Seven – We humbly ask God to remove our shortcomings.

PERSONALIZED: I humbly ask God to remove my shortcomings.

Memorize

Keep the process simple: Keep It Simple Stupid (KISS).

Internalize

Motivational Thought

Internalize the fact that you need to use God's Word to fight against condemning feelings or doubts whenever they occur.

6

Health

When it comes to our health, we often separate our physical state from our spiritual and mental state. In order for us to be healthy on the outside, we must be healthy on the inside, spiritually and mentally. We need to have a healthy body in order to allow God to effectively work through us. Just as in any other area of our life, such as money, family, and relationships, God expects us to be wise stewards of our bodies. In I Corinthians 3:16, Paul declares, "Do you not know that you are the temple of God and that the Spirit of God dwells in you?" (NKJV). It is important to remember that the Holy Spirit has come to live in the heart and life of every believer. It is imperative that we care for our body by eating healthily and exercising regularly. If we do not take care of ourselves, it becomes difficult to care for those around us.

Health

Scriptures

Job 12:10 (NKJV)

"In whose hand is the life of every living thing, and the breath of all mankind?"

Proverbs 3:7–8 (NKJV)

"Do not be wise in your own eyes; fear the Lord and depart from evil. It will be health to your flesh, and strength to your bones."

Proverbs 4:20–22 (NKJV)

"My son, give attention to my words; incline your ear to my sayings. Do not let them depart from your eyes; keep them in the midst of your heart; for they are life to those who find them, and health to all their flesh."

Proverbs 15:30 (NKJV)

"The light of the eyes rejoices the heart, and a good report makes the bones healthy."

Proverbs 17:22 (NKJV)

"A merry heart does good, like medicine, but a broken spirit dries the bones."

Matthew 6:27 (NKJV)

"Which of you by worrying can add one cubit to his stature?"

1 Corinthians 6:19–20 (NKJV)

"Or do you not know that your body is the temple of the Holy Spirit, who is in you, whom you have from God, and you are

not your own? For you were brought at a price; therefore glorify God in your body and in your spirit, which are God's."

Steps of the Twelve Steps

One – We admitted that we are powerless over alcohol, and that our lives had become unmanageable.

Two – We came to believe that a Power greater than ourselves could restore us to sanity.

Three – We made a decision to turn our will and our lives over to the care of God as we understood Him.

Four – We made a searching and fearless moral inventory of ourselves.

Eleven – We sought, through prayer and meditation, to improve our conscious contact with God as we understood Him, praying only for knowledge of His will and the power to carry it out.

Personalize

The personalization continues. As stated earlier, use "I," "my," and "me" statements. Continue to use these when appropriate, and make it yours. Also keep in mind that when you are personalizing, change in the scripture or step may not always occur. If it sounds good the way it is written, personalize it that way.

Scriptures (Personalized)

Job 12:10 (NKJV)

"In whose hand is the life of every living thing, and the breath of all mankind?"

PERSONALIZED: The life of every living thing is in His hand, as is the breath of all mankind.

Proverbs 3:7–8 (NKJV)

"Do not be wise in your own eyes; fear the Lord and depart from evil. It will be health to your flesh, and strength to your bones."

PERSONALIZED: I will not be wise in my own eyes; I will hear the Lord and depart from evil. It will be health to my flesh and strength to my bones.

Proverbs 4:20–22 (NKJV)

"My son, give attention to my words; incline your ear to my sayings. Do not let them depart from your eyes; keep them in the midst of your heart; for they are life to those who find them and health to all their flesh."

PERSONALIZED: I will pay attention and listen carefully to what God says. I will not lose sight of His words. I will allow the words to penetrate deep within my heart, for they bring life and radiant health as I discover their meaning.

Proverbs 15:30 (NKJV)

"A light of the eyes rejoices the heart, And a good report makes the bones healthy."

PERSONALIZED: A cheerful look brings joy to my heart; and good news makes for good health.

Proverbs 17:22 (NKJV)

"A merry heart does good, like medicine, But a broken spirit dries the bones."

PERSONALIZED: A cheerful heart is good medicine; but a broken spirit saps my strength.

Matthew 6:27 (NKJV)

"Which of you by worrying can add one cubit to his stature?"

PERSONALIZED: Worrying will not add one cubit to my stature.

1 Corinthians 6:19 (NKJV)

"Or do you not know that your body is the temple of the Holy Spirit, who is in you, whom you have from God, and you are not your own?"

PERSONALIZED: I know that my body is the temple of the Holy Spirit, who is in me, whom I have from God, and I am not my own.

Steps of the Twelve Steps (Personalized)

One – We admitted that we are powerless over alcohol, and that our lives had become unmanageable.

PERSONALIZED: I admit that I am powerless over my **health**, and that my life has become unmanageable.

Two – We came to believe that a Power greater than ourselves could restore us to sanity.

PERSONALIZED: I have come to believe that only a Power that is greater than me can restore my health.

Three – We made a decision to turn our will and our lives over to the care of God as we understand Him.

PERSONALIZED: I have made a conscious decision to turn my health over to God as I understand Him to be.

Four – We made a searching and fearless moral inventory of ourselves.

PERSONALIZED: I have made a fearless moral inventory of who I am.

Eleven – We sought, through prayer and meditation, to improve our conscious contact with God as we understand Him, praying only for knowledge of His will for us and the power to carry that out.

PERSONALIZED: I have sought, through prayer and meditation, to improve my relationship with God in order for His will to be more effectively carried out in my life.

Memorize

By now, you may have chosen your method; if not, let me suggest one at this point. Try to remember by association. This particular process involves both what you already know and what you want to remember. Whatever it is that you are trying to remember, associate it with something you already know, visualizing it in your mind.

Internalizing is happening

Motivational Thought

"Or do you not know that your body is the temple of the Holy Spirit who is in you, whom you have from God, and you are not your own?" (1 Corinthians 6:19, NKJV)

Steps of the Twelve Steps (Personalized)

One – We admitted that we are powerless over alcohol, and that our lives had become unmanageable.

PERSONALIZED: I admit that I am powerless over my **health**, and that my life has become unmanageable.

Two – We came to believe that a Power greater than ourselves could restore us to sanity.

PERSONALIZED: I have come to believe that only a Power that is greater than me can restore my health.

Three – We made a decision to turn our will and our lives over to the care of God as we understand Him.

PERSONALIZED: I have made a conscious decision to turn my health over to God as I understand Him to be.

Four – We made a searching and fearless moral inventory of ourselves.

PERSONALIZED: I have made a fearless moral inventory of who I am.

Eleven – We sought, through prayer and meditation, to improve our conscious contact with God as we understand Him, praying only for knowledge of His will for us and the power to carry that out.

PERSONALIZED: I have sought, through prayer and meditation, to improve my relationship with God in order for His will to be more effectively carried out in my life.

Memorize

By now, you may have chosen your method; if not, let me suggest one at this point. Try to remember by association. This particular process involves both what you already know and what you want to remember. Whatever it is that you are trying to remember, associate it with something you already know, visualizing it in your mind.

Internalizing is happening

Motivational Thought

"Or do you not know that your body is the temple of the Holy Spirit who is in you, whom you have from God, and you are not your own?" (1 Corinthians 6:19, NKJV)

7

Finances

Most Americans struggle with finances. We are not taught how to manage our finances, and the last place we look for answers is in the Word. I too succumbed to the consequences of poor decision-making regarding finances. I found budgeting my money to be very bothersome, and tracking my monthly expenses was as far as I went. I finally realized that without budgeting my money, I would be in a continuous cycle of debt, always owing someone, a slave to my debtors. I also realized that this was not the way God wanted me to live. Hebrews 13:5 states "Let your conduct be without covetousness; be content with such things as you have. For He Himself has said, "I will never leave you nor forsake you." (NKJV). As challenging as it was, I did it. I was blessed with a new financial beginning, and I started listening to and obeying what God was saying regarding my financial situation. The results have been amazing.

Finances

Scriptures

Proverbs 3:9 (NKJV)

"Honor the Lord with your possessions, And with the firstfruits of all your increase;"

Proverbs 10:4 (NKJV)

"He who has a slack hand becomes poor, But the hand of the diligent makes rich."

Proverbs 13:11 (NKJV)

"Wealth gained by dishonesty will be diminished, But he who gathers by labor will increase."

Matthew 6:21 (NKJV)

"For where your treasure is, there your heart will be also."

Luke 14:28 (NKJV)

"Suppose one of you wants to build a tower. Won't you first sit down and estimate the cost to see if you have enough money to complete it?"

1 Timothy 6:10 (NKJV)

"For the love of money is a root of all kinds of evil, for which some have strayed from the faith in their greediness, and pierced themselves through with many sorrows."

Hebrews 13:5 (NKJV)

"Keep your lives free from the love of money and be content with what you have, because God has said, 'Never will I leave you, never will I forsake you.'"

Steps of the Twelve Steps

One – We admitted that we are powerless over our addiction, and that our lives had become unmanageable.

Two – We came to believe that a Power greater than ourselves could restore us to sanity.

Five – We admitted to God, to ourselves, and to another human being the exact nature of our wrongs.

Personalize

Let's do it again. Personalize it, and make it yours.

Scriptures (Personalized)

Proverbs 3:9 (NKJV)

"Honor the Lord with your possessions, And with the firstfruits of all your increase;"

PERSONALIZED: I will honor the Lord with my wealth and with the best part of everything I produce.

Proverbs 10:4 (NKJV)

"He who has a slack hand becomes poor, But the hand of the diligent makes rich."

PERSONALIZED: Lazy hands will make me poor, but diligent hands will bring me wealth.

Proverbs 13:11 (NKJV)

"Wealth gained by dishonesty will be diminished, But he who gathers by labor will increase."

PERSONALIZED: Dishonest money dwindles away, but gathering money little by little will make it grow.

Matthew 6:21 (NKJV)

"For where your treasure is, there your heart will be also."

PERSONALIZED: Where my treasure is, there my heart will be also.

Luke 14:28 (NKJV)

"For which of you, intending to build a tower, does not sit down first and count the cost, whether he has enough to finish it?"

PERSONALIZED: Suppose I want to build a tower. Will I not first sit down and estimate the cost to see if I have enough money to complete it?

1 Timothy 6:10 (NKJV)

"For the love of money is a root of all kinds of evil, for which some have strayed from the faith in their greediness, and pierced themselves through with many sorrows."

PERSONALIZED: For the love of money is a root of all kinds of evil, for which some have strayed from the faith in their greediness, and pierced themselves through with many sorrows.

Hebrews 13:5 (NKJV)

"Let your conduct be without covetousness; be content with such things as you have. For He himself has said, "I will never leave you nor forsake you."

PERSONALIZED: I will keep free from the love of money and be content with what I have, because God has said, "Never will I leave you, and never will I forsake you."

Steps of the Twelve Steps (Personalized)

One – We admitted that we are powerless over our addiction, and that our lives had become unmanageable.

PERSONALIZED: I admit that I am powerless over my **finances**, and that my life has become unmanageable.

Two – We came to believe that a Power greater than ourselves could restore us to sanity.

PERSONALIZED: I have come to believe that only a Power that is greater than me can restore my finances.

Five – We admitted to God, to ourselves, and to another human being the exact nature of our wrongs.

PERSONALIZED: I have admitted to God, to myself, and to another person(s) the exact nature of my wrongs.

Memorize

Our memory is a powerful thing! Keep on moving on, and remember: "garbage in, garbage out." What you put in is what you will get out.

Internalizing is happening

Motivational Thought

Speak God's Word over your finances; this will produce growth and abundance. As you work through your finances and investments, remember that the best investments will be in your spiritual growth.

8
Substance Abuse (Drugs/Alcohol)

Whether you believe addiction is a disease /illness or a choice, it does not change the fact that it needs to be dealt with. Out of the many clients I have worked with, most believe that it is both a choice and a disease. Those who believe it is a choice struggle with answering the question, "Once people cross the gates back into the community, why do they relapse?" Is it then *your choice* to start to drink or use again? Is the disease in remission?

The clients who I work with are incarcerated, and have thus abstained from using for a considerable amount of time. They have not used because it is (supposedly) not available. For this reason, I often ask them, "Why, then, would you make the choice to start to use again? What do you feel would cause or contribute to your relapse?" As you would suspect, there are a wide range of answers—many of which led to the writing of this book. Upon listening to the many responses, the common thread was that there were many other challenges in other areas of their lives that had not been addressed.

In my teachings, I discuss how issues in one area can spill over into other areas, thus creating a domino effect. I have taught my clients that the way an individual **thinks**, the way they **feel**, their **environment**, and their **beliefs** determine their

behaviors. At the end of the day, they have to make choices (good or bad), and there are consequences to whatever decisions they make. So in some regards they have choices, but it is always more complicated than that. It takes more than just saying no. They need something or someone to say *yes* to. My suggestion is that since they have tried everything else; why not say yes to God?

Addiction

Scriptures

Proverbs 3:5–6 (NKJV)

"Trust in the Lord with all your heart, and lean not on your own understanding; in all your ways acknowledge him, and He shall direct your paths."

Romans 12:1 (NKJV)

"I beseech you therefore, brethren, by the mercies of God, that you present your bodies a living sacrifice, holy, acceptable to God, which is your reasonable service."

1 Corinthians 10:13 (NKJV)

"No temptation has overtaken you except such as is common to man; but God is faithful, who will not allow you to be tempted beyond what you are able, but with the temptation will also make the way of escape, that you may be able to bear it."

2 Corinthians 5:17 (NKJV)

"Therefore, if anyone is in Christ, he is a new creation; old things have passed away; behold, all things have become new."

Philippians 2:13 (NKJV)

"For it is God who works in you both to will and to do for His good pleasure."

Philippians 4:13 (NKJV)

"I can do all this through Christ who strengthens me."

James 1:22 (NKJV)

"But be doers of the word, and not hears only, deceiving yourselves."

Steps of the Twelve Steps

One – We admitted that we were powerless over our addiction, and that our lives had become unmanageable.

Two – We came to believe that a Power greater than ourselves could restore us to sanity.

Three – We made a decision to turn our will and our lives over to the care of God as we understand Him.

Four – We made a searching and fearless moral inventory of ourselves.

Five – We admitted to God, to ourselves, and to another human being the exact nature of our wrongs.

Six – We were entirely ready to have God remove all these defects of our character.

Seven – We humbly asked Him to remove our shortcomings.

Eight – We made a list of all persons we had harmed, and become willing to make amends to them all.

Nine – We made direct amends to such people whenever possible, except when to do so would injure them or others.

Ten – We continued to take a personal inventory, and when we were wrong, we promptly admitted it.

Eleven – We sought, through prayer and meditation, to improve our conscious contact with God as we understood Him, praying only for knowledge of His will for us and the power to carry that out.

Twelve – Having had a spiritual awakening as the result of these steps, we tried to carry this message to alcoholics, and to practice these principles in all our affairs.

Personalize

Scriptures (Personalized)

Proverbs 3:5–6 (NKJV)

"Trust in the Lord with all your heart, and lean not on your understanding; in all your ways acknowledge him, and he shall direct your paths."

PERSONALIZED: I will trust in the Lord with all my heart, and lean not on my own understanding; in all my ways I will acknowledge Him, and He will direct my paths.

Romans 12:1 (NKJV)

"I beseech you therefore, brethren, by the mercies of God, that you present your bodies a living sacrifice, holy, acceptable to God, which is your reasonable service."

PERSONALIZED: In view of God's mercy, I will offer my body as a living sacrifice, holy and pleasing to God; this is my spiritual act of worship.

1 Corinthians 10:13 (NKJV)

"No temptation has overtaken you except such as is common to man; but God is faithful, who will not allow you to be tempted beyond what you able, but with the temptation will also make the way of escape, that you may be able to bear it."

PERSONALIZED: No temptation has seized me except what is common to man. And God is so faithful; He will not let me be tempted beyond what I can bear. But when I am tempted, He will also provide a way out so that I can stand up under it.

2 Corinthians 5:17 (NKJV)

"Therefore, if anyone is in Christ, he is a new creation; old things have passed away; behold, all things have become new."

PERSONALIZED: Therefore, if I am in Christ, I am a new creation; the old has gone, the new has come!

Philippians 2:13 (NKJV)

"For it is God who works in you both to will and to do for His good pleasure."

PERSONALIZED: For it is God who works in me both to will and to do for His good pleasure.

Philippians 4:13 (NJKV)

"I can do all this through Christ who strengthens me."

PERSONALIZED: I can do all things through Christ who strengthens me.

James 1:22 (NKJV)

"But be doers of the word, and not hearers only, deceiving yourselves."

PERSONALIZED: I should not just listen to the word, deceiving myself; I should do what it says.

Steps of the Twelve Steps (Personalized)

One – We admitted that we are powerless over our addiction, and that our lives had become unmanageable.

PERSONALIZED: I admit that I am powerless over the use of the **Twelve Steps**, and that my life has become unmanageable.

Two – We came to believe that only a Power that is greater than ourselves can restore our life back to a normal state of being.

PERSONALIZED: I have come to believe that only a Power greater than myself can restore my life back to a normal state of being.

Romans 12:1 (NKJV)

"I beseech you therefore, brethren, by the mercies of God, that you present your bodies a living sacrifice, holy, acceptable to God, which is your reasonable service."

PERSONALIZED: In view of God's mercy, I will offer my body as a living sacrifice, holy and pleasing to God; this is my spiritual act of worship.

1 Corinthians 10:13 (NKJV)

"No temptation has overtaken you except such as is common to man; but God is faithful, who will not allow you to be tempted beyond what you able, but with the temptation will also make the way of escape, that you may be able to bear it."

PERSONALIZED: No temptation has seized me except what is common to man. And God is so faithful; He will not let me be tempted beyond what I can bear. But when I am tempted, He will also provide a way out so that I can stand up under it.

2 Corinthians 5:17 (NKJV)

"Therefore, if anyone is in Christ, he is a new creation; old things have passed away; behold, all things have become new."

PERSONALIZED: Therefore, if I am in Christ, I am a new creation; the old has gone, the new has come!

Philippians 2:13 (NKJV)

"For it is God who works in you both to will and to do for His good pleasure."

PERSONALIZED: For it is God who works in me both to will and to do for His good pleasure.

Philippians 4:13 (NJKV)

"I can do all this through Christ who strengthens me."

PERSONALIZED: I can do all things through Christ who strengthens me.

James 1:22 (NKJV)

"But be doers of the word, and not hearers only, deceiving yourselves."

PERSONALIZED: I should not just listen to the word, deceiving myself; I should do what it says.

Steps of the Twelve Steps (Personalized)

One – We admitted that we are powerless over our addiction, and that our lives had become unmanageable.

PERSONALIZED: I admit that I am powerless over the use of the **Twelve Steps**, and that my life has become unmanageable.

Two – We came to believe that only a Power that is greater than ourselves can restore our life back to a normal state of being.

PERSONALIZED: I have come to believe that only a Power greater than myself can restore my life back to a normal state of being.

Three – We have made a conscious decision to turn both our will and our lives over to God as we understand who God is.

PERSONALIZED: I have made a conscious decision to turn both my will and my life over to God as I understand who God is.

Four – We made a searching and fearless moral inventory of who we are.

PERSONALIZED: I have made a searching and fearless moral inventory of who I am.

Five – We admitted to God, to ourselves, and to another human being the exact nature of our wrongs.

PERSONALIZED: I have admitted to God, to myself, and to another human being the exact nature of my wrongs.

Six – We were entirely ready to have God remove all these defects of our character.

PERSONALIZED: I am ready to have God remove all the defects of my character.

Seven – We humbly ask Him to remove our shortcomings.

PERSONALIZED: I will humbly ask Him to remove my shortcomings.

Eight – We made a list of all of the persons we had harmed, and become willing to make amends to them all.

PERSONALIZED: I will make a list of all people I have hurt as a result of my problem, and am willing to make amends to each and every person on the list.

Nine – We made amends to such people whenever possible, except when to do so would injure them or others.

PERSONALIZED: I will make amends to each person whenever it is possible, except in cases where to do so would cause more injury to the person in question or other people.

Ten – We continued to take a personal inventory, and when we were wrong, we promptly admitted it.

PERSONALIZED: I will continue to take a personal inventory of myself on a regular basis, and when I am at fault, I will be willing to admit it.

Eleven – We sought, through prayer and meditation, to improve our conscious contact with God as we understood Him, praying only for knowledge of His will for us and the power to carry that out.

PERSONALIZED: I will seek, through prayer and meditation, to improve my relationship with God as I understand Him, praying for knowledge of His will for me and the power to carry out.

Twelve – All eleven steps have provided a spiritual awakening, and as a result, we have made it our mission to bring the message of recovery to others and to practice these principles in everything we do.

PERSONALIZED: All eleven steps have provided a spiritual awakening, and as a result, I have made it my mission to bring the message of recovery to others and to practice these principles in everything I do.

Memorize

As stated earlier, the mind is a powerful tool. All we have to do is feed it information. The mind is a terrible thing to waste.

Internalizing is happening

Motivational Thought

Remember, as you internalize information, it is what you shall become.

9

Goal Setting

Have you ever considered where you want to be in the next ten, twenty, or thirty years? Given our high-tech world and fast-paced society, we often find ourselves too busy to consider setting goals. Other reasons why we don't set goals are that they are too long-range, we don't see immediate results, they may not be realistic, or they may not be specific enough. Instead of setting a course of action to get where we want, we often go wherever the day takes us, driven by our emotions. With no goals, our lives just become a drift.

We are all here for a reason, and we are to live our lives with purpose. We all have things that we want to accomplish, thus giving our life meaning. We all need to set goals. It is important to know where you are going, and to have a plan of how to get there. My hope is that you will understand that we all need goals to work toward in life.

Below is an example of goal setting and achievement. Study and follow the steps. Discipline and commitment will go hand and hand with setting goals.

Goal Setting

Goal setting is an important method of:

- deciding what is important to you
- separating what is important to you from what is irrelevant
- motivating yourself to achievement
- building self-confidence

You should allow yourself to enjoy the achievement of your goals; reward yourself appropriately.

Goal Setting Steps

Step 1 – Desire is the great motivation, a powerful force that drives you toward your goals.

Step 2 – You must **believe** with all your heart, and have no doubts that you have the ability to achieve your goals.

Step 3 – The third and most important step is to **write** your goals out in complete detail, exactly as you wish to have them. Until your goals are committed to paper, they are not goals; they are simply wishes backed by fantasies.

Step 4– Determine the **benefits** you will receive by achieving your goals. Write out all of the benefits you will enjoy after accomplishing your goals.

Step 5 – Set a deadline. Decide exactly when you are going to accomplish your goals, and put it down on paper.

Step 6 – Identify the **obstacles** you will have to overcome to achieve your goals.

Step 7 – Clearly define the **knowledge** you will need in order to accomplish your goals.

Step 8 – Take all of the details that you have identified in steps 6 and 7, and create a **plan of action**. Be sure to make it complete with every little detail.

Step 9 – Get a clear **mental picture** of your goals, as if they are already attained. Repeatedly picture yourself succeeding and achieving your goals. Let your imagination run wild!

Step 10 – Back up you plan with **determination, persistence**, and a burning desire to never, never give up until you have achieved your goal.

Additional Tips

- Make sure the goal you are working for is something you really want, not just something that sounds good.
- If you need help from someone to achieve your goal, will you have his or her cooperation?
- Write your goal with positive language rather than negative language. Work for what you want, not for what you want to leave behind.
- Write your goal out in complete detail.
- Make sure your goal is ambitious enough.
- Reviewing your goals daily or weekly is crucial to your success; this must become a part of your routine. Each morning after you wake up, read your list of goals aloud. Visualize the completed goal: see the new home, smell the leather seats in your new car,

feel the new smaller outfit on your body. Each night before you go to bed, repeat this process. This process will jump-start both your subconscious and conscious mind to work toward your goal. This will also replace any negative self-talk with positive self-talk.

Scriptures

Psalm 25:9 (NKJV)

"The humble He guides in justice, and the humble He teaches His way."

Psalm 32:8 (NKJV)

"I will instruct you and teach you in the way you should go."

Psalm 37:23 (NKJV)

"The steps of a good man are ordered by the Lord, and He delights in his way."

Psalm 73:24 (NKJV)

"You will guide me with Your counsel, and afterward receive me to glory."

Psalm 121:8 (NKJV)

"The Lord shall preserve your going out and your coming in from this time forth, and even forevermore."

Proverbs 3:5–6 (NKJV)

"Trust in the Lord with all your heart, and lean not on your own understanding."

Isaiah 30:21 (NKJV)

"Your ears shall hear a word behind you, saying, 'This is the way, walk in it,' whenever you turn to the right hand or whenever you turn to the left."

Steps of the Twelve Steps

One – We admitted that we are powerless over our addiction, and that our lives had become unmanageable.

Two – We come to believe that a Power greater than ourselves could restore us to sanity.

Three – We made a decision to turn our will and our lives over to the care God as we understand Him.

Seven – We humbly asked Him to remove our shortcomings.

Eleven – We sought, through prayer and meditation, to improve our conscious contact with God as we understood Him, praying only for knowledge of His will for us and the power to carry that out.

Personalize

Scriptures (Personalized)

Psalm 25:9 (NKJV)

"The humble He guides in justice, and the humble He teaches His way."

PERSONALIZED: I will be guided in justice and taught His ways.

Psalm 32:8 (NKJV)

"I will instruct you and teach you in the way you should go."

PERSONALIZED: He will instruct me and teach me in the way I should go.

Psalm 37:23 (NKJV)

"The steps of a good man are ordered by the Lord, and He delights in his way."

PERSONALIZED: The steps of a good man are ordered by the Lord, and He delights in his way.

Psalm 73:24 (NKJV)

"You will guide me with Your counsel, and afterward receive me to glory."

PERSONALIZED: He will guide me with His counsel, and afterward will receive me to glory.

Psalm 121:8 (NKJV)

"The Lord shall preserve your going out and your coming in from this time forth, and even forevermore."

PERSONALIZED: The Lord will preserve my going out and my coming in, from this time forth and even forevermore.

Proverbs 3:5–6 (NKJV)

"Trust in the Lord with all your heart, and lean not on your own understanding."

PERSONALIZED: I will trust in the Lord with all my heart, and lean not on my own understanding.

Isaiah 30:21 (NKJV)

"Your ears shall hear a word behind you, saying, 'This is the way, walk in it,' whenever you turn to the right hand or whenever you turn to the left."

PERSONALIZED: My ears shall hear a word behind me saying, "This is the way, walk in it," whenever I turn to the right hand or whenever I turn to the left hand."

Steps of the Twelve Steps (Personalized)

One – We admitted that we were powerless over our alcohol, and that our lives had become unmanageable.

PERSONALIZED: I admit that I am powerless over the **goal**s that have been set for my life, and that my life has become unmanageable.

Two – We came to believe that a Power greater than ourselves could restore us to sanity.

PERSONALIZED: I have come to believe that a Power greater than myself can restore me to sanity.

Three – We made a decision to turn our will and our lives over to the care of God as we understand Him.

PERSONALIZED: I have made a decision to turn my will and life over to the care of God as I understand Him.

Seven – We humbly asked Him to remove our shortcomings.

PERSONALIZED: I have humbly asked Him to remove my shortcomings.

Eleven – We sought, through prayer and meditation, to improve our conscious contact with God as we understood Him, praying only for knowledge of His will for us and the power to carry that out.

PERSONALIZED: I will seek, through prayer and meditation, to improve my relationship with God as I understand Him, praying for knowledge of His will for me and the power to carry it out.

Memorize

Hopefully by now you are experiencing how powerful your memory is. Part of the ability to memorize is understanding what you are memorizing. As you memorize, take some time to think about what you are committing to memory.

Internalizing is happening

Motivational Thought

What you are personalizing and internalizing by memorization will become a part of you.

Conclusion

You have made it to the end! It is my prayer that you are delivered from whatever issues you battle with in life. Throughout the process, I hope you have come to understand what James 4:8 states: "Draw near to God and He will draw near to you" (NKJV). Working on any area in your life requires determination, commitment, and patience. Whatever your desire or goal in life is, it is attainable. Allow Him into your heart and life. God bless!

WORK SHEET

TOPIC

_____

Scripture to topic	Twelve Steps to the topic

WORK SHEET

TOPIC

_____

Scripture to topic　　　　　**Twelve Steps to the topic**

Goal Setting

WORK SHEET

TOPIC

_____

Scripture to topic   **Twelve Steps to the topic**

WORK SHEET

TOPIC

_____

Scripture to topic   **Twelve Steps to the topic**

www.ingramcontent.com/pod-product-compliance
Ingram Content Group UK Ltd.
Pitfield, Milton Keynes, MK11 3LW, UK
UKHW022217230426
12048UKWH00016BA/894